©2010 Paperback ISBN: 978-0-635-07508-6
©2010 Library Binding ISBN: 978-0-635-07552-9

Gallopade is proud to be a member of these educational organizations and associations:

American Library Association (ALA)
The National School Supply and Equipment Association (NSSEA)
The National Council for the Social Studies (NCSS)
National Association for Gifted Children (NAGC)
American Booksellers Association (ABA)
Museum Store Association (MSA)
International Reading Association (IRA)
Supporter of **Association of Partners for Public Lands (APPL)**

Published by
GALLOPADE™ INTERNATIONAL
800-536-2GET
www.gallopade.com

CAROLE MARSH BOOKS

Other Carole Marsh Books

Orville & Wilbur Wright . . . Step Out Into The Sky!
Lewis & Clark Go On a Hike: The Story of the Corps of Discovery
The Louisiana Purchase: "What A Deal!"
The American Revolution: How Our Nation Was Born
The American Civil War: When Brother Fought Brother
The U.S. Civil Rights Movement: The Fight For Equality
The Bill of Rights: "It Can't Be Wrong!"
U.S. Constitution: "Sign on the Dotted Line!"
The Declaration of Independence: "Quit Bossing Us Around!"
Jamestown: America's First Permanent English Settlement
The Underground Railroad: Path to Freedom
Industrial Revolution: From Muscles to Machines!
Great Depression & the New Deal: Brother, Can You Spare a Dime?
World War II: When Men, Women, and Children Saved the World
Brown v. Board of Education: I Want to Go to School!
World War I: The War to End All Wars!
Abraham Lincoln: America's 16th President
The U.S. Supreme Court: The Keepers of the Laws of Our Land
Galloping West with the Pony Express!: "The Mail Must Go Through!"
The Transcontinental Railroad: The Big Race to the Golden Spike!
The 13 Colonies: A New Life in a New World!
Wagons Ho! Pioneers' Path to the West!: The Oregon Trail

State Stuff™, Available for all 50 states:

My First Pocket Guide
State My First Book
State Wheel of Fortune Gamebook
State Survivor Gamebook
State Illustrated Timelines
"Jography!": A Fun Run Through Our State
The State Coloring Book
The Big Reproducible Activity Book
State Millionaire Gamebook
State Project Books
Jeopardy: Answers & Questions About Our State

Patriotic Favorites™

Patriotic Favorites Coloring Book
Patriotic Biographies
The Daily Patriot: 365 Quotations
Young Patriots Coloring & Activity Book
Patriotic Projects
Patriotisms: 365 Definitions

Table of Contents

A Word from the Author

Dear Reader,

I am fascinated by the brave pioneers who settled this country! Sometimes I wonder if I would have been one of them traveling west before railroads, cars, or airplanes. Would I have packed all of my belongings into a small wagon? Would I have said goodbye to my extended family, knowing I probably would never see them again? Would I have been able to travel in a wagon for months and months?

Thousands of average people like you and me were brave enough to cross the Oregon Trail. It was a terribly long journey with lots of bumps along the way—wild animals, Indian attacks, sickness, accidents—not to mention running out of food or getting stuck in a blinding winter blizzard! But to them, starting a new life in the West was worth it!

So many traveled the Oregon Trail that the wagon wheels cut deep ruts into the earth. Some of the ruts can still be seen today. They stand as a silent reminder of the sacrifice and determination of the westward pioneers. What an incredible example they are of the American spirit!

I hope you enjoy learning about the Oregon Trail as much as I did writing this book. If we pay attention and learn from it, history is a wonderful teacher!

Wagons Ho!

Carole Marsh

A Timeline of Events

1804 President Thomas Jefferson assigns Meriwether Lewis and William Clark to explore the West.

1805 Lewis and Clark arrive in Oregon at the end of their long exploration.

1829 The American Society for Encouraging the Settlement of the Oregon Territory is organized.

1836 Marcus and Narcissa Whitman are the first white settlers in Oregon.

1843 The year of the "Great Migration." Large numbers of settlers begin traveling west. Also known as the "Wagon Train of 1843."

1848 The "Oregon Country" becomes a United States territory.

1849 Gold is discovered in California. Many "Forty Niners" head west to make a fortune.

1850 The Oregon Donation Land Act is created. It offers free land to settlers who travel west.

1859 Congress welcomes Oregon as the 33rd state.

1869 The Union and Pacific railroads are connected at Promontory Summit, Utah. The railroads connect the East and West, and provide an easier way to travel.

Wagons Ho! Pioneers' Path to the West!:

The Oregon Trail

On a warm spring day in Independence, Missouri, hundreds of Americans scurry around town gathering supplies for a momentous journey. On the edge of town, rows of wooden wagons stand at attention, covered with half-moons of canvas that look like sails. The year is 1843. Anxious pioneers yearn to travel west, and this is their launching point on the Oregon Trail.

Each wagon will soon embark on a journey that will last through the summer months. They will rumble over flat prairies, struggle across raging rivers, and climb steep mountains. Their riders will walk countless miles and sleep in the open prairie along the way. Many dangers await them in the unknown. But at the end of the trail lies Oregon—a land of new beginnings!

Get There Sooner with a Prairie Schooner!

The pioneers needed the right kind of wagon to travel to the West. It had to carry lots of supplies. It had to be able to roll on flat, rocky, and soggy ground. It had to be strong enough to last through months of travel. Regular flat, wooden horse wagons were not sturdy enough.

The solution was the Conestoga wagon, also known as a "covered wagon." It had a wooden bottom and a large, white, curved "bonnet" on the top. The bonnet on top of the wagon gave pioneers shade and protected them from rain and storms.

The Conestoga wagon had huge wheels that could roll over almost any type of land. The wagon was made from thick wooden planks. Tar stuffed between the planks kept out the water and wind. The wagon was perfect for traveling the Oregon Trail. People started calling these special wagons "prairie schooners" because they looked like sail boats floating across the prairie! Can't you just picture it?

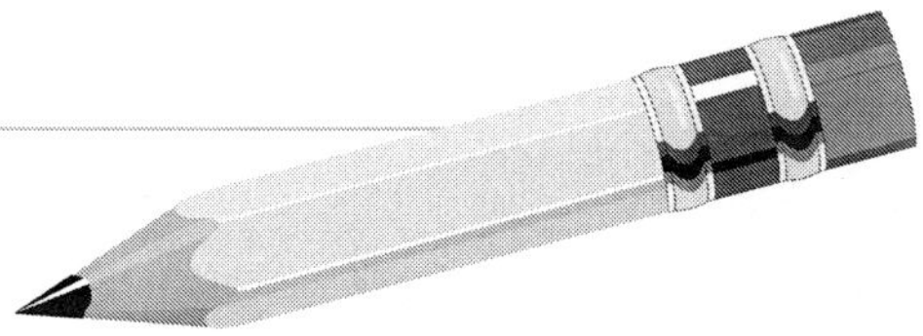

Make a Covered Wagon!

Materials:

1 pint size milk carton
markers (brown and black)
tape
white construction paper
four milk lids

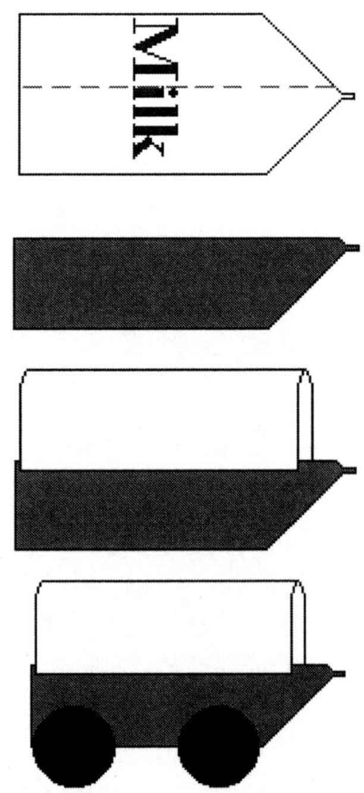

Directions:

1. Cut the milk carton in half longways.

2. Lay the cut carton on its side and color it brown with your markers (you can use paint if you have it!).

3. Paint the four milk lids black for your wheels.

4. Cut out a piece of construction paper about 8" by 5". Tape it over the half of the milk carton in a loop shape.

5. Glue the wheels in place and you have your very own prairie schooner!

What's in That Wagon?

The pioneers needed many supplies for their journey. They were moving from one house, all the way across the country, to another. Today, we use big trucks to move our furniture, clothes, toys, and other goods. The pioneers had a wagon that was only 10 feet long by 4 feet wide. That's not a lot of room!

Pioneers had to pack wisely in order to make the most of the space. They had to think about everything they packed. Would it be useful? Could they live without it? Would they miss it once they got to the West? It must have been hard trying to pack for a place they'd never seen. They didn't even have a computer to check the weather or look at pictures of Oregon on the Internet!

To Bring or Not to Bring!

Here are some of the many things a pioneer family might choose to take with them on their journey west. Circle the items you think *do not* belong on this list.

TOOLS

ax
hammer
shovel
rope
tractor
animal trap
automatic nail gun

HOUSEHOLD GOODS

Dutch oven
butter churn
mirror
laptop computer
wooden bucket
table and chairs
cooking utensils
dishes
clock
toaster oven
DVD player

PERSONAL ITEMS

dolls
books
iPod
family Bible
fiddle

You Are What You Eat

Food took up the most space in a wagon. In fact, a family of four would have to pack 1,000 pounds of food to last the journey! Remember, on the prairie they didn't have microwaves, refrigerators, toasters, or freezers. They had to bring food that would not go bad along the way.

Pioneers had to think long and hard about what food they would bring. If they brought too much, the wagon would be too heavy for the oxen to pull. If they didn't bring enough, they risked running out of food in the middle of the prairie.

Pioneers chose supplies like coffee, sugar, flour, salt, and dried beans because they would not spoil. Bacon was the most popular meat to bring on the Oregon Trail. It was easy to store because it was cured and lasted a long time. Pioneers usually bought 150 pounds of bacon before starting their journey! They hunted animals along the trail for other meats.

Do the Math!

Answer the following math questions to make sure your pioneers have enough food for their journey.

1 If a family of four eats 1 pound of bacon a day, how many pounds will they need for 40 days?

____

2 Joe, a brave pioneer, is halfway across the Oregon Trail, but he only has 3 pounds of flour left. If one batch of biscuits uses one-fourth of a pound of flour, how many batches of biscuits can he make?

____

3 Papa hunted a deer on the trail and he now has fresh steaks for his family! Papa has 8 steaks from the deer. Without a refrigerator, the meat will last only 4 days. If Papa divides the steaks evenly each day, how many steaks will Papa's family have to eat each day so that no steaks go bad?

____

4 After she stocked up on food at the supply store, Abigail realized her wagon was too heavy! She bought 156 pounds of food but her wagon can only hold 140 pounds of food. How many pounds of food will Abigail have to give away to another family?

____

Fashion on the Prairie

Pioneer clothing was more practical than fashionable. Most of the pioneers' clothes were not bought at a store. Mothers and daughters knew how to sew and made all the clothes for their families. They made the clothes out of fabrics like wool, calico, and flannel because those materials were cheap.

There wasn't much room for clothes in a wagon. The pioneers needed space in the wagon for other important things. That meant that each person in a family only had a couple of items of clothing. Women wore big skirts and boots. Men wore thick long pants and button-up shirts. If a man's shirt got dirty, he kept on wearing it! If his pants ripped, his wife fixed them!

Ready to Wear!

Match each item of clothing to the correct word below.

1. _______ wool pants

2. _______ bonnet

3. _______ men's flannel shirt

4. _______ wool skirt

5. _______ men's boots

6. _______ women's flannel blouse

7. _______ women's boots

8. _______ wool coat

a.

g.

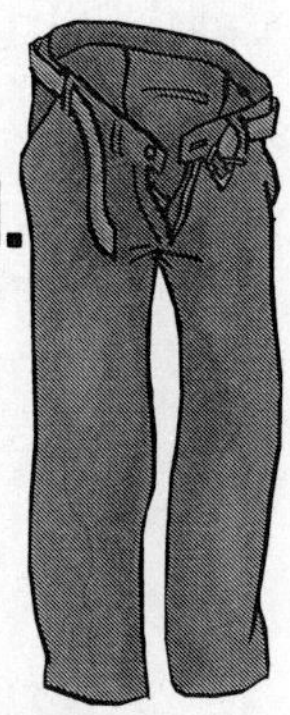
d.

c.

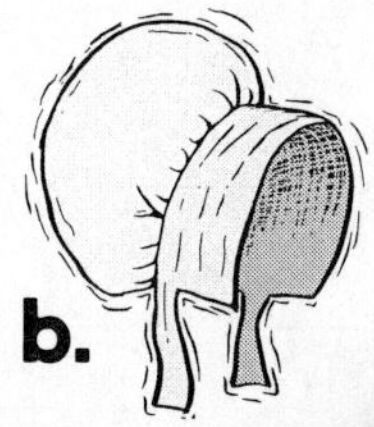
b.

h.

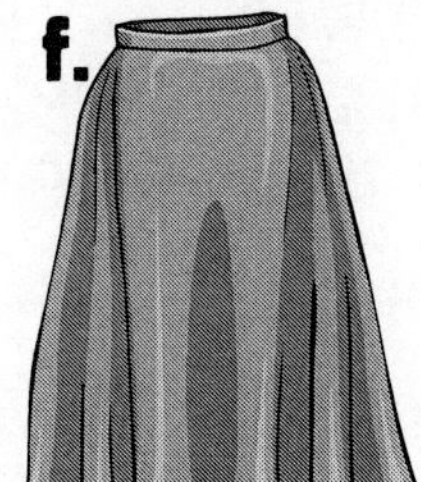
f.

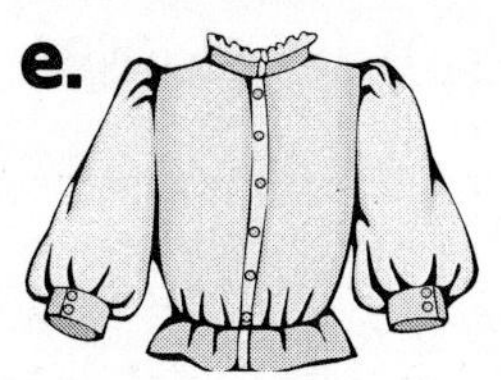
e.

Mules, Horses, and Oxen, OH MY!

Once the pioneers packed their wagon to the brim with supplies, they needed one more important member for their journey. An ox! Oxen are a special type of cow that are very big, but very slow. The oxen were so slow on the trail that most wagons only moved a few miles every hour. Kids on the Oregon Trail could usually walk faster than their wagons!

The pioneers chose oxen over horses and mules because of their great strength. Although a horse could run much faster than an ox, the pioneers quickly found out that horses were not strong enough to pull a wagon on the Oregon Trail.

However, horses were still useful on the Oregon Trail. Pioneers rode them beside the wagons and used them for hunting. Plus, they needed something to ride once they got to their new home—no one wants to ride around town on a cow!

Animal Assets!

The pioneers may have chosen oxen, but what do you think? Look at the pros and cons of oxen, horses, and mules. Write any additional pros and cons you can think of for each in the blanks below.

Horses	**Mules**	**Oxen**
Pros	**Pros**	**Pros**
Fast	Strong	Very strong
Easy to ride	Faster than oxen	No special care
______________	______________	______________
______________	______________	______________
Cons	**Cons**	**Cons**
Need lots of food and water	Can be stubborn	Slow
	Can be lazy	______________
______________	______________	______________
______________	______________	

Write a paragraph about which animal you would choose to pull your wagon across the Oregon Trail. Why did you choose that animal?

____

____

____

____

Who Were Those Pioneers?

Over the years, thousands of pioneers went to Oregon. Most of them traveled west to make a new life. In many ways, the pioneers were like the first pilgrims who sailed many miles across the ocean to settle in America. They were brave to make a dangerous journey to a new land. Without the brave pioneers, we may have never discovered the wonderful things in the West.

Pioneers were brave, strong, smart, and independent. Most of all, they were normal people just like you and me! They were farmers, doctors, lawyers, missionaries, blacksmiths, mothers, shopkeepers, and children. They were regular Americans from the eastern United States!

Do You Have What It Takes?

Circle the words below that describe a pioneer on the Oregon Trail.

DETERMINED

PATIENT BRAVE ORGANIZED

LAZY QUITTER

OPTIMISTIC MOTIVATED

CONFIDENT INTELLIGENT

CURIOUS

FOOLISH COMPLAINER

FEARFUL

FAST FACT! The first pioneers to make a home in Oregon were Marcus and Narcissa Whitman. They were missionaries from New York. The Whitmans spent many years sharing their religion with the Indians in Oregon.

Let's Get Ready to Roll!

Before the pioneers set foot in Independence, Missouri, they had lots of preparation to do. Sure, they had to pack the wagon, feed the oxen, and buy food. But the pioneers also had to plan which way they were going to travel—there weren't too many maps back then!

The pioneers needed to make sure they left Independence during the spring so they wouldn't get caught in the cold winter snow. They had to think about important questions like: What dangerous rivers were they going to cross? What would they do if a wagon wheel broke? What would they do if someone got sick? What would happen once they got to Oregon?

It took a LOT of work to prepare for life on the Oregon Trail!

Moving On!

Independence, Missouri marked the beginning of the Oregon Trail. But many pioneers traveled a long way just to get to Independence! Using the map, answer the questions below.

1. If Pioneer John was traveling from New York to Independence, Missouri, through how many states would he travel? (including New York) ______________
2. From Independence, Missouri, how many states would a pioneer have to travel through on the Oregon Trail to get to Oregon City, Oregon? ____________
3. How many states did Pioneer John have to travel through to get from New York City, New York to Oregon City, Oregon? _________________

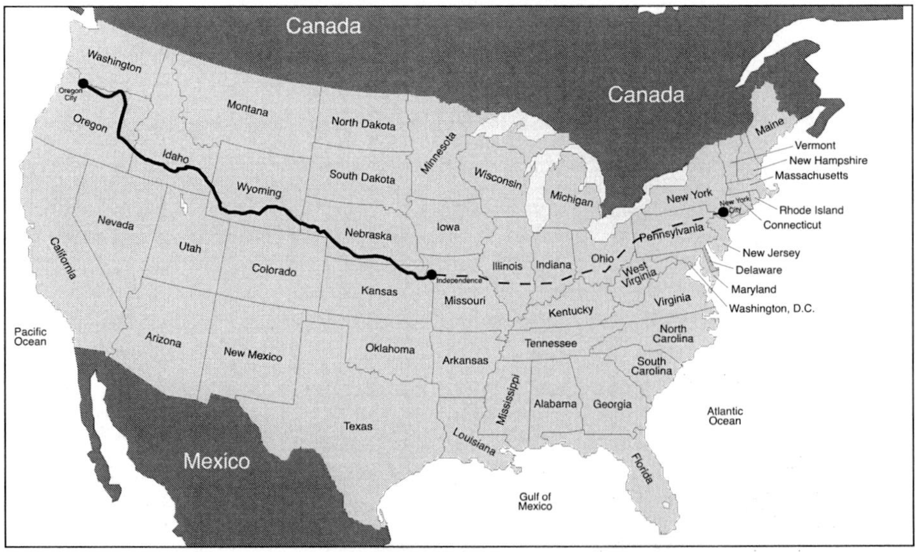

Manifest Destiny

In the 1840s, America was growing quickly. The original 13 colonies were filling up with people. American leaders knew they had to find more land for their growing country.

At that time, many believed it was America's mission to travel west and discover new land. Some wanted to bring democracy, America's form of government, to the Indians in the West. Others wanted to bring their religion to the Indians. Many wanted the United States to have more land.

American leaders used the term "Manifest Destiny" to talk about the growth of America. They believed that it was America's destiny to explore the West. In the 1840s, Manifest Destiny was a popular topic in political speeches and newspaper articles all over the country.

Learn About It!

Look up and write the definitions for the words below. Then, put the definitions together to help you better understand the meaning of Manifest Destiny.

manifest:

____

____

destiny:

____

____

Read the list of reasons someone might want to travel west below. Write MD next to each one that describes why someone who believed in Manifest Destiny, or expanding west, would want to go west.

1. ________ To hunt buffalo
2. ________ To spread religion to the Indians
3. ________ To have a party
4. ________ To make friends with the Indians
5. ________ To find more land for America
6. ________ To spread democracy to the Indians
7. ________ To find a nice place for a vacation
8. ________ To start a new life

Mapping Out the Oregon Trail

Have you ever wondered how the Oregon Trail got started? Who decided where to go? Why couldn't the pioneers get to Oregon another way?

The path of the Oregon Trail was carefully planned out. Mapmakers and explorers traveled west before the pioneers. They found the safest trail to the West. It followed the easiest places to cross rivers. It also led the wagons through the Rocky Mountains. The mountains were dangerous because wagons could fall off steep cliffs, break their wheels, or get stuck between rocks. The Oregon Trail led wagons through one of the only places in the Rocky Mountains where they could safely cross.

Some pioneers decided to take a risk and not take the Oregon Trail. They formed other popular trails like the Mormon Trail that led to Utah, and the California Trail that led to California.

Figure It Out!

Answer the following math questions to learn more about just how long a journey the pioneers had.

1. If a wagon travels 2 miles per hour, how many miles will it travel in 8 hours?

   __________________.

2. If a wagon travels 20 miles each day, how many miles will it travel in one week?

   __________________.

3. If a wagon travels 20 miles each day, how many days will it take the wagon to travel the full 2,000 miles of the Oregon Trail?

   __________________.

4. Using your answer from Question 3, about how many months would it take the same wagon to cross the Oregon Trail?

   __________________.

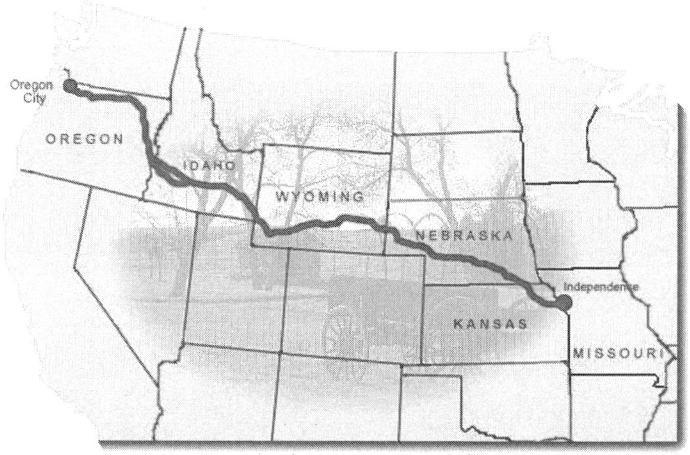

Perils Along the Trail

There were many serious dangers on the Oregon Trail. Many people died on their journey west. The most common dangers were river crossings, sickness, wagon accidents, and gun accidents.

Sadly, many pioneers drowned when they tried to cross a river with their wagon. The rivers were deep and the water moved fast. Wagons and people could be swept away by the river's current.

Sickness also killed many people on the Oregon Trail. The most common disease was cholera. There was no cure for cholera. It made people very sick very fast.

Wagon accidents were also dangerous for the pioneers. Wagons could tip over or roll down a steep hill. The most common wagon accident was a person being crushed under the huge wagon wheels. Many children were killed along the trail when they got caught under the heavy, moving wagon wheels. Surprisingly, some pioneers were hurt or killed by accidental gun shots!

Make a Compass!

It could be very dangerous if a pioneer got lost on the way to Oregon. To make sure your pioneers are headed west, make your own compass from these simple materials.

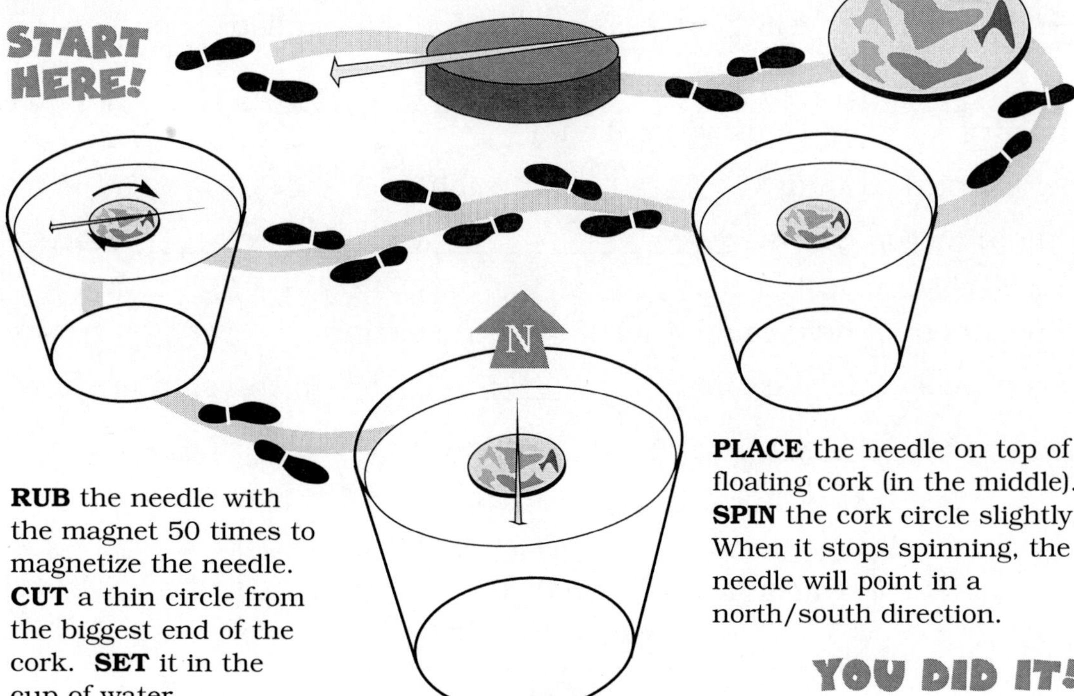

RUB the needle with the magnet 50 times to magnetize the needle. **CUT** a thin circle from the biggest end of the cork. **SET** it in the cup of water.

PLACE the needle on top of the floating cork (in the middle). **SPIN** the cork circle slightly. When it stops spinning, the needle will point in a north/south direction.

All Aboard the Wagon Train

The pioneers quickly learned that it wasn't smart to travel the Oregon Trail alone. If their wagon broke or someone got sick, they were stuck. But if the pioneers traveled in groups, they could help each other. So, they started the wagon train as a safer and faster way to get to Oregon than traveling alone.

The group was called a wagon train because all the wagons traveled in a straight line, one behind the other. From far away, it looked like a train!

A wagon master usually led the wagon train. He knew important things about the trail. He decided where the train would stop at night, which rivers they would cross, and how many miles they should travel in one day.

Each wagon train did the same thing every day. They got up before the sun rose, loaded their wagons, and started rolling. They stopped for an hour for lunch. They kept rolling until dark. When the day's travels were done, they corralled their wagons, or lined them up in a circle. They did this to protect the wagons from intruders and keep their animals from running away.

Test Your Knowledge!

Fill in the blanks below with the correct answer from the Word Bank.

1. A group of wagons traveling on the Oregon Trail was called a

   ____________ ____________.
2. The leader of a wagon train was called a ____________ ____________.
3. The wagons parked in a ____________ at night.
4. Traveling in wagon trains was ____________ and ____________ than traveling alone.
5. The pioneers could help each other if they traveled in ____________.
6. The wagon master decided how many ____________ to travel in one day.

Word Bank

faster	circle	safer
wagon train	miles	groups
	wagon master	

The Legend of the West—Buffalo!

One of the most fascinating mysteries of the West was the great buffalo. Pioneers heard stories about the giant animals that traveled in massive herds across the Great Plains. One early explorer said the plains "were black and appeared as if in motion" with the buffalo herds. And when the pioneers got there, they saw that the stories were true! Some said they saw more than one million buffalo in one herd!

To see a buffalo in real life was exciting for the pioneers. Most hunted the buffalo for sport. The pioneers would chase the buffalo, kill them, and leave their bodies in the prairie. Thousands of buffalo were killed by pioneers just for fun. So many animals died that buffalo are endangered today. You can no longer see the huge herds of millions of buffalo rumbling across the prairie.

FAST FACT! Buffalo poop was hard to avoid on the Oregon Trail! Once it dried, the buffalo poop, or chips, as the pioneers called them, could be used for fuel in fires. Pioneer kids even played games tossing around the flat buffalo chips!

Write a Poem!

Read the poem below about the fate of the buffalo. Then write your own poem.

Buffalo Dusk

by Carl Sandburg

THE BUFFALOES are gone.
And those who saw the buffaloes are gone.
Those who saw the buffaloes by thousands
and how they pawed the prairie sod into
dust with their hoofs, their great heads
down pawing on in a great pageant of
dusk,
Those who saw the buffaloes are gone.
And the buffaloes are gone.

At the Next Rock, Turn Left!

Most of the Oregon Trail was flat land, but every once in a while, a special landmark rose out of the prairie. Landmarks were very exciting for pioneers. They let them know they were closer to Oregon. Landmarks also helped pioneers stay on the trail. They knew which direction to go and how far they should travel to the next landmark.

Independence Rock

Some landmarks were so beautiful that wagon trains stopped to take a break and enjoy the scenery. Some of the most popular landmarks were massive rocks looming in the middle of the prairie. Chimney Rock, Jail Rock, Courthouse Rock, and Independence Rock were popular stops.

Lasting Landmarks!

Look at the map of some of the landmarks on the Oregon Trail. Circle the correct answers below.

1. What is the first landmark a pioneer would see after they leave Independence, Missouri?
   a. The Dalles b. Courthouse and Jail Rock c. Oregon City

2. Once a pioneer reached Courthouse and Jail Rock, what is the next landmark they would see?
   a. Independence, MO b. Independence Rock c. Chimney Rock

3. What is the last landmark a pioneer would pass before reaching Oregon City?
   a. Independence Rock b. The Dalles c. Independence, MO

4. Independence Rock is ______________ of the Oregon Trail.
   a. in the middle b. at the beginning c. at the end

Writing on the Rock

Independence Rock is one of the most famous landmarks on the Oregon Trail. When pioneers saw the rock, they knew they were halfway across the trail. The rock is called Independence because most pioneers reached the rock around the 4th of July. The pioneers celebrated when they finally saw the huge rock in the distance!

Independence Rock is also special because the pioneers carved and painted things on the rock. They signed their names, wrote dates, and wrote notes to friends who were traveling behind them. Most of the writing on the rock has faded over time, but some names carved into the rock can still be seen today!

Leave Your Mark!

Use the space below to write on Independence Rock. Sign your name, write the date, and leave a note for someone traveling behind you.

Indians—The First Pioneers

The Indians lived in the West before any pioneers traveled along the Oregon Trail. The Plains Indians lived off of the prairie. They hunted buffalo. Unlike the white pioneers, the Indians hunted buffalo for food. They used every part of the buffalo—the meat, fur, and bones. Nothing was wasted.

Many people think the Indians attacked and killed the white pioneers. In fact, more pioneers died from accidental gun shot wounds than from Indian attacks. Many Indians even helped the pioneers survive the Oregon Trail.

The pioneers that came to the West changed the lives of Indians forever. Before the pioneers arrived, between 40 and 60 million buffalo roamed the land. As the buffalo began dying, the Indians had nothing to hunt for food and shelter. Eventually, the Indians were forced off their land and sent to reservations. Reservations are pieces of land set aside for Indians.

It's Time!

Put the timeline below in order. Label the events 1-5 where 1 is the event that happened first and 5 is the event that happened last.

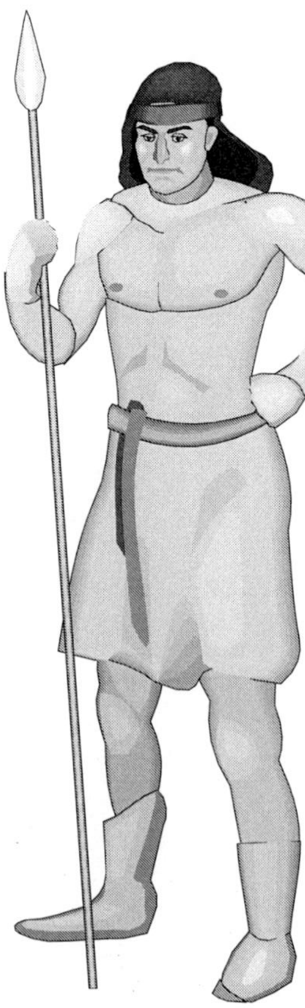

Indians live on reservations

☐

Pioneers begin to move west on Oregon Trail

☐

Indians settle in the West

☐

Some Indians help the pioneers on Oregon Trail

☐

Too many buffalo killed by pioneers

☐

Journal Your Journey!

Many pioneers kept a personal journal of their travels on the Oregon Trail. They talked about how they felt, what they saw, and what dangers they experienced. Some of those journals have been turned into books that you can read today.

The journals helped other pioneers understand how to make the journey. They also help people today understand what the pioneers experienced on the Oregon Trail.

Write It!

Write your own journal entry about a day on the Oregon Trail. Be sure to let your reader see, hear, taste, feel, and smell the world you describe. You might want to talk about a landmark you see, a danger you have faced, or how you feel about your trip.

Date: ____________

Name: ____________________________

____

____

____

____

____

____

____

____

____

Quick Draw!

Along with journals, many pioneers on the Oregon Trail kept sketch books. They drew all the new things they saw around them. They often drew detailed pictures of famous landmarks.

Draw It!

Pretend you are a pioneer. Draw a picture of something you experienced on the Oregon Trail in your sketch book below. You can draw the clothes people wore, the animals you saw, or a famous landmark. Be sure to make your drawing as detailed as possible.

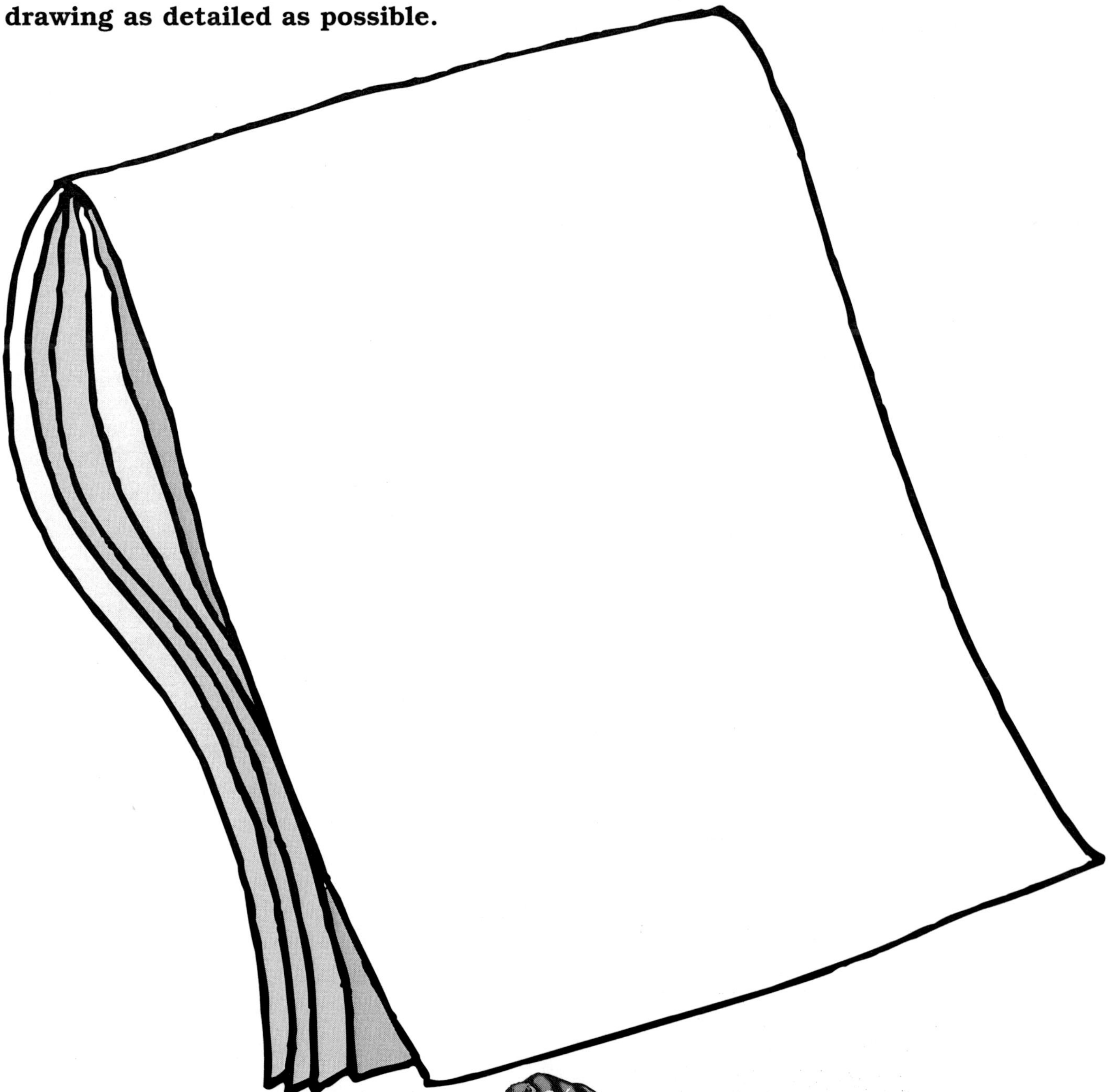

Home, Sweet Home—Finally!

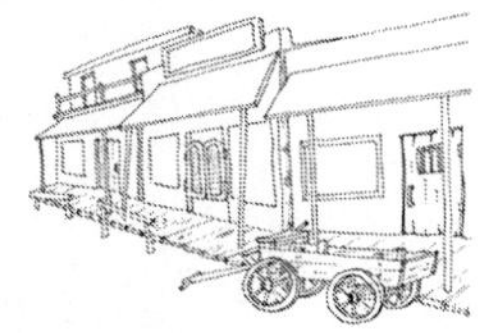

When the weary pioneers saw Oregon City for the first time, they were delighted! After months and months, they were so glad to see a thriving town! One emigrant said, "We were happy, after a long and tedious tour, to witness the home of civilization. To see mills, storehouses, shops. To hear the noise of the workman's hammer; to enjoy the warm welcome of countrymen and friends." Those who survived the journey celebrated their success. They finally had hope of a new life!

Spread the News!

Help the pioneers celebrate the end of the Oregon Trail by designing the front page of your own newspaper! Write an article about the pioneers' journey on the Oregon Trail.

1. Masthead (Name of newspaper-make one up!)
2. Date Happened (Write on this line.)
3. Dateline (Place where happened)
4. BIG HEADLINE!
5. Tell the news!
6. Photo (Draw a picture of a covered wagon in the box.)
7. Sidebar (Put a quotation or trivia fact in lower right box.)
8. Editor (Hey, that's you!)

Additional Resources

BOOKS

Fantastic Facts about the Oregon Trail by Michael J. Trinklein
The Oregon Trail by Elaine Landau
Journal of Travels: Over the Oregon Trail in 1845 by Reuben Gold Thwaites
The Oregon Trail Sketches of Prairie and Rocky-Mountain Life by Francis Parkman
The Tragic Tale of Narcissa Whitman and a Faithful History of the Oregon Trail by Cheryl Harness

WEBSITES

The Oregon Trail
http://www.isu.edu/~trinmich/Allabout.html

End of the Oregon Trail Interpretive Center
http://www.historicoregoncity.org/HOC/index.php?option=com_content&view=category&id=75&Itemid=80/

The Oregon Trail, produced by History Globe
http://www.historyglobe.com/ot/otmap1.htm

MUSEUMS

End of the Oregon Trail Interpretive Center, Oregon City, Oregon
Museum of Western Expansion, St. Louis, Missouri

Glossary

blacksmith: someone who shapes iron with heat and a hammer

calico: plain, cotton fabric

cholera: bacterial disease contracted through contaminated drinking water; symptoms include vomiting, stomach cramps, and diarrhea

endurance: the ability to get through hard situations

expansion: making something bigger

herd: a group of animals that roam together

momentous: very important; of great significance

peril: great danger

pilgrims: the colonists from England who came to America on the Mayflower

pioneer: the first people to explore and settle on a piece of land

prairie: a flat land with no trees and lots of grass

Answer Key

Page 9: tractor, automatic nail gun, laptop computer, toaster oven, DVD player, iPod

Page 10: 1. 40; 2. 12; 3. 2; 4. 16

Page 11: 1. d; 2. b; 3. h; 4. f; 5. a; 6. e; 7. c; 8. g

Page 13: brave, patient, optimistic, confident, curious, intelligent, motivated, organized, determined

Page 14: 1. 6; 2. 6; 3. 12

Page 15: 2, 5, 6, 8

Page 16: 1. 16 miles; 2. 140 miles; 3. 100 days; 4. about 3

Page 18: 1. wagon train; 2. wagon master; 3. circle; 4. faster, safer; 5. groups; 6. miles

Page 20: 1. b; 2. c; 3. b; 4. a

Page 22: 5, 2, 1, 3, 4

Index